I0420634

Copyright © 2015 Quote Octopus.com

Quote Octopus
Melbourne, Victoria, 3053
Australia
www.quoteoctopus.com

Creative without strategy is called 'art.' Creative with strategy is called 'advertising.'

Jef I. Richards

Transforming a brand into a socially responsible leader doesn't happen overnight by simply writing new marketing and advertising strategies. It takes effort to identify a vision that your customers will find credible and aligned with their values.

Simon Mainwaring

Good advertising does not just circulate information. It penetrates the public mind with desires and belief.

Leo Burnett

Advertising is the art of convincing people to spend money they don't have for something they don't need.

Will Rogers

I believe that life is hard. That we all are going to walk through things that are hard and challenging, and yet advertising wants us to believe that it's all easy.

Jamie Lee Curtis

Many a small thing has been made large by the right kind of advertising.

Mark Twain

When the Internet first came into public use, it was hailed as a liberation from conformity, a floating world ruled by passion, creativity, innovation and freedom of information. When it was hijacked first by advertising and then by commerce, it seemed like it had been fully co-opted and brought into line with human greed and ambition.

Neil Strauss

I know that campaigns can seem small, and even silly. Trivial things become big distractions. Serious issues become sound bites. And the truth gets buried under an avalanche of money and advertising. If you're sick of hearing me approve this message, believe me - so am I.

Barack Obama

Advertising works most effectively when it's in line with what people are already trying to do. And people are trying to communicate in a certain way on Facebook - they share information with their friends, they learn about what their friends are doing - so there's really a whole new opportunity for a new type of advertising model within that.

Mark Zuckerberg

It takes a big idea to attract the attention of consumers and get them to buy your product. Unless your advertising contains a big idea, it will pass like a ship in the night. I doubt if more than one campaign in a hundred contains a big idea.

David Ogilvy

Advertising is the greatest art form of the 20th century.

Marshall McLuhan

The more informative your advertising, the more persuasive it will be.

David Ogilvy

The most powerful element in advertising is the truth.

William Bernbach

Advertising is fundamentally persuasion and persuasion happens to be not a science, but an art.

William Bernbach

Never stop testing, and your advertising will never stop improving.

David Ogilvy

Americans born since World War II have grown up in a media-saturated environment. From childhood, we have developed a sort of advertising literacy, which combines appreciation for technique with skepticism about motives. We respond to ads with at least as much rhetorical intelligence as we apply to any other form of persuasion.

Virginia Postrel

Half the money I spend on advertising is wasted; the trouble is, I don't know which half.

John Wanamaker

Starbucks is not an advertiser; people think we are a great marketing company, but in fact we spend very little money on marketing and more money on training our people than advertising.

Howard Schultz

When governments rely increasingly on sophisticated public relations agencies, public debate disappears and is replaced by competing propaganda campaigns, with all the accompanying deceits. Advertising isn't about truth or fairness or rationality, but about mobilising deeper and more primitive layers of the human mind.

Brian Eno

It takes more than capital to swing business. You've got to have the A. I. D. degree to get by - Advertising, Initiative, and Dynamics.

Isaac Asimov

Google was founded to get information to everybody. A by-product of that strategy is that we invented an advertising business which has provided great economics that allows us to build the servers, hire the employees, create value.

Eric Schmidt

Young people are threatened... by the evil use of advertising techniques that stimulate the natural inclination to avoid hard work by promising the immediate satisfaction of every desire.

Pope John Paul II

What really decides consumers to buy or not to buy is the content of your advertising, not its form.

David Ogilvy

If you ever have the good fortune to create a great advertising campaign, you will soon see another agency steal it. This is irritating, but don't let it worry you; nobody has ever built a brand by imitating somebody else's advertising.

David Ogilvy

In advertising not to be different is virtually suicidal.

William Bernbach

I always say it took me 10 minutes to write 'Cars,' but if I am honest it could have been even less than that - and it has been a really successful song over the years. It is still massively used, in advertising, in films, and people do cover versions of it a lot.

Gary Numan

The critic is the only independent source of information. The rest is advertising.

Pauline Kael

Advertising is the 'wonder' in Wonder Bread.

Jef I. Richards

The interesting thing about advertising is that the things that annoy us sometimes about it are really human. It's us looking at ourselves - and like all human endeavors it's imperfect.

Jaron Lanier

As the mainstream media has become increasingly dependent on advertising revenues for support, it has become an anti-democratic force in society.

Robert McChesney

I've always been scared of advertising folk. I've met them at parties and I've been to their offices and I've always found them intimidatingly cool. At one company I visited, they held their meetings in a caravan that had somehow been installed in the place, a rather more exotic place to gather than the typical BBC glass box.

Evan Davis

In advertising, sex sells. But only if you're selling sex.

Jef I. Richards

The thinner a newspaper or magazine is - due to reduced revenue from advertising dollars - the less editorial content because of the standard ad-to-editorial ratio, and the less money there is to support investigative journalism.

Lynda Resnick

People don't understand the logistics of advertising.

Susan Wojcicki

I believe in advertisement and media completely. My art and my personal life are based in it. I think that the art world would probably be a tremendous reservoir for everybody involved in advertising.

Jeff Koons

The printed newspaper is a powerful showcase for news, opinion and advertising.

Jill Abramson

Advertising at its worst will be killed by the Internet. And rightly so.

Maurice Saatchi

There is no rivalry between Google and traditional advertising.

Maurice Saatchi

The most common trouble with advertising is that it tries too hard to impress people.

James Randolph Adams

If you have a business website, make it stickier; redo the merchandising often and try new things until you hit the right homepage... then try and beat that. The most important audience drivers on the Internet are paid search and key word optimization. Concentrate on those. They are very inexpensive compared to banner advertising.

Lynda Resnick

A viewer who skips the advertising is the moral equivalent of a shoplifter.

Nicholas Johnson

An enormous amount of direct advertising from pharmaceutical companies are offering a kind of instantaneous solution to problems.

Leon Kass

Advertising - a judicious mixture of flattery and threats.

Northrop Frye

Advertising is very simple in a lot of ways. Advertisers go where the users go, and users are choosing to spend a lot more time online.

Susan Wojcicki

Advertising was fairly simple work, and I really just wanted a job where I could sit and write every day and not get fired for it like I had at other jobs, but it was fun.

John Hughes

I went out to some advertising agencies and asked if I could do anything.

Renny Harlin

We knew when we started the Daily Muse, we wanted a recruiting-focused business model rather than an advertising-focused one. We felt like publishers were being forced to go to more and more extreme lengths to monetize through advertising.

Kathryn Minshew

The number of small businesses in the United States totals about 25 million. Because most of these have a local trading territory, relatively few advertise online. Online advertising reaches the masses of the Internet world, whether they are local or not.

Marc Ostrofsky

Advertising is the principal reason why the business man has come to inherit the earth.

James Randolph Adams

Ninety-five percent of the time when I run a contest I've purchased the giveaway prizes with advertising money.

Ree Drummond

Art work is inconclusive. It opens your mind up. At least, that's what I hope it does. And advertising, using exactly the same photograph, closes things down. It makes it conclusive. It sells a product, and that is its primary function.

Alison Jackson

If its not done ethically, advertising won't be trusted. If consumers don't trust it, advertising is pointless.

Jef I. Richards

Google and Facebook, each in their own way, have revolutionized the delivery of advertising based on search and social networking, creating a sort of anti-Spam: targeted, relevant ads that a consumer might actually welcome rather than spurn.

Marcus Buckingham

Sales may lead to advertising as much as advertising leads to sales.

Michael Schudson

When it went on the air, the sales department hated it. It was the highest advertising pullout show in the history of NBC. At the early focus groups, people were saying, 'Who are these people? Why should we watch them?

Dick Wolf

There are plenty of people who are willing to pay $2.6 million for 30 seconds on the Super Bowl and hundreds of thousands of dollars for 'American Idol.' There will be advertising dollars on the Internet. We're there as well. We win either way.

Leslie Moonves

I decided to go to school for advertising and graphic design. That was what I was gonna do but acting is that thing, it's like a splinter in your mind and you can't get rid of it. So I decided to move to L.A. a few years ago and it just snowballed into this thing called 'The Hunger Games.'

Dayo Okeniyi

Everybody's enamored of the iPhone, the Google phone. But the applications are going to change. You know, we're going to start using our phones for shopping. It's going to change the nature of advertising.

Tim O'Reilly

Extension work is not exhortation. Nor is it exploitation of the people, or advertising of an institution, or publicity work for securing students. It is a plain, earnest, and continuous effort to meet the needs of the people on their own farms and in the localities.

Liberty Hyde Bailey

All media owners want to attract advertising revenue. Google is no different.

Maurice Saatchi

I have learned that you can't have good advertising without a good client, that you can't keep a good client without good advertising, and no client will ever buy better advertising than he understands or has an appetite for.

Leo Burnett

CBS is the largest out-of-home advertising company in the U.S.

Leslie Moonves

We inside Diesel are the first consumers of our advertising. We make ad campaigns for our own amusement - that's why they succeed.

Renzo Rosso

If we listen human instinct actually tells us what we need, but advertising makes us want things we don't need and things we can't have.

Kit Williams

Advertising is speech. It's regulated because it's often effective speech.

Jef I. Richards

I was in advertising for years. That was cushy, you know? It's pretty cushy in a lot of ways, but I hated it.

Augusten Burroughs

Critics say Internet advertising suffers from limitless inventory, which depresses prices. These exclusive front-page sponsorships are not limitless. If HBO doesn't move quickly enough, Showtime can buy out Gawker and Jezebel for the key fall TV season. On any individual day, there isn't room for both of them; and that's healthy.

Nick Denton

Advertising holding companies used to boast about their share of the advertising market. Now they are proud of how much of their business is not in advertising.

Maurice Saatchi

The time has come when advertising in some hands has reached the status of a science.

Claude C. Hopkins

The online musical universe has become Balkanized, with many sites focusing on minute niches. That works well for reaching very specific demographics, which is wonderful for advertising, but it flies in the face of the common wisdom that people's tastes have become more diverse as music of any description has become a mouse-click away.

Michael Azerrad

But I think technology advertising will have to stop addressing how products are made and concentrate more on what a product will do for the consumer.

Jay Chiat

We are all advertising, all of the time. If you want to sell your car, what do you do? You clean and polish it and make it the best you can. Some people bake bread when they are trying to sell their house because the smell adds a friendly feeling. Even the priest, with all his or her fervour, is advertising God. Everybody is selling.

Paul Arden

Is advertising a profession, like law or medicine? How many new parents clutch their baby to their breast and declare, 'I want this child to grow up to be a media planner'?

Jef I. Richards

The Death of Advertising? I think that's in the book of Revelation. It's the day when people everywhere become satisfied with their weight, their hair, their skin, their wardrobe, and their aroma.

Jef I. Richards

I've always been a fan of advertising, I've always been a fan of television, I've loved commercials, I've loved all the jingles, I loved all the stuff.

Jon Hamm

It is not the purpose of the ad or commercial to make the reader or listener say, 'My what a clever ad.' It is the purpose of advertising to make the reader say, 'I believe I'll buy one when I'm shopping tomorrow'.

Morris Hite

Mass consumption, advertising, and mass art are a corporate Frankenstein; while they reinforce the system, they also undermine it.

Ellen Willis

Client companies and advertising agencies are old-world-order places. The systems and processes and structures come from a time when you shot the TV commercial, then you did the print ads, then you did everything else - including the website. Everything has changed, but the systems haven't.

Cindy Gallop

When I give talks like the one I'm going to give at the Changing Advertising Summit, one of the points I often make to the audience is that I'm not one of those speakers who stands in front of the audience and pontificates - everything I talk about I'm actually doing myself. I'm living it.

Cindy Gallop

The engine of ancient society was religion but the engine of contemporary society, as I see it, is advertising.

Kit Williams

Why, I ask, isn't it possible that advertising as a whole is a fantastic fraud, presenting an image of America taken seriously by no one, least of all by the advertising men who create it?

David Riesman

You have always had individual directors who begin in the advertising or commercial world, but they are probably exceptions rather than the traditional pattern.

Ann Macbeth

My mum is very political - left wing - and my dad was in the advertising business. They were both from the East Coast: Boston and New York City, respectively.

Joan Cusack

The Internet offers an interesting combination of advertising and community by participating in the community you can become an advertisement for yourself.

Walter Jon Williams

Advertising ought to work by telling you what it is you want to tell, you should understand what you want us to do, what you want us to think, where you want us to shop.

Jay Chiat

And it's interesting, when you look at the predictions made during the peak of the boom in the 1990s, about e-commerce, or internet traffic, or broadband adoption, or internet advertising, they were all right - they were just wrong in time.

Chris Anderson

In my opinion, fun is what makes advertising successful.

Leo Bogart

Everything is about color. If you look at magazines and advertising and television, the thing you remember is the color.

Kelly Wearstler

Advertising degrades the people it appeals to; it deprives them of their will to choose.

Carrie Snow

Advertising is what you do when you can't go see somebody. That's all it is.

Fairfax Cone

The effectiveness of advertising depends on the amount and kind of product information available to consumers... advertising will be more successful the more impoverished the consumer's information environment.

Michael Schudson

I long for the day when advertising will become a business for a grown man.

Howard Gossage

The first law in advertising is to avoid the concrete promise... and cultivate the delightfully vague.

John C. Crosby

I'm not in the advertising business, but I think it would be very nice if people went to see the film Hamlet, because it was made with love and integrity.

Julie Christie

You can't make money on advertising; you just have to seed the clouds. What you're after is word of mouth.

Mitch Leigh

I've come up through art school, through painting, through graphic design, through advertising, through TV commercials and music video. I've designed books, built billboards, matchbooks, corporate identities. I continuously paint, I've done conceptual art pictures.

Tony Kaye

The vast majority of Americans agree with us. We're doing everything that we can. We're advertising, right now we're on television with an advertisement running in the Washington area. We've got newspaper ads.

Michael D. Barnes

There is no such thing as a Mass Mind. The Mass Audience is made up of individuals, and good advertising is written always from one person to another. When it is aimed at millions it rarely moves anyone.

Fairfax Cone

A magazine is simply a device to induce people to read advertising.

James Collins

My father did advertising photography.

Andreas Gursky

Television is more of a business. You can't take as many risks, because there's so many channels now, and the advertising's dropping.

Dana Delany

No one wakes up excited to see more advertising, no one goes to sleep thinking about the ads they'll see tomorrow.

Jan Koum

When advertising is involved, you, the user, are the product.

Jan Koum

One of the challenges of buying local advertising is, how do you know if it worked? How do you know if it's got value? We're moving toward an e-commerce experience for local, an Amazon-like experience for local.

Jeremy Stoppelman

Obama was 200 percent advertising. I promote myself to sell my brands. Because now I am a kind of celeb. I am in a different world than the fashion industry. I am with Mick Jagger, Michael Jackson, Madonna. I build me as a celebrity.

Christian Audigier

I believe that a contract, or at least an understanding, exists between the American public and the American advertiser concerning what advertising is, what its limitations are and what price people will pay for it.

John O'Toole

A lot of kids do not know my club exists yet. I did not do any big advertising, and that's what I might do in the next two or three weeks, put something in the paper.

Thomas Dooley

If there are signs that Americans bow to the gods of advertising, there are equally indications that people find the gods ridiculous. It is part of the popular culture that advertisements are silly.

Michael Schudson

Some people are averse to change, but the advertising model is going to change with or without the Hopper. What we're saying to the broadcasters is, 'There's a way for you not to put your head in the sand.'

Charlie Ergen

There is no such thing as national advertising. All advertising is local and personal. It's one man or woman reading one newspaper in the kitchen or watching TV in the den.

Morris Hite

Mahalo's business model is advertising. Yahoo, Google, Ask, AOL and MSN are all advertising-based. So I don't see anything wrong with advertising-based search.

Jason Calacanis

It is the growth of advertising in this country which, more than any single element, has brought the American magazine to its present enviable position in points of literary, illustrative and mechanical excellence.

Edward Bok

Magazines and advertising are flogging the idea that you have to keep changing things and get something new. I think that's balls - evil. But obviously that's your livelihood.

Robin Day

If you look at the heritage of the best advertising, you can make stuff that is great for both readers and advertisers. I don't think Don Draper would have loved banner ads.

Jonah Peretti

Advertising is a wonderful lubricant for business, if it's used properly.

John Cullum

The world is changing... I don't, as a consumer, want advertising that's not relevant. If we're going to take a side, let's take the side of the consumer.

Charlie Ergen

I think mobile advertising is going to be huge.

Matt Cohler

Citigroup has the opportunity to be the largest financial institution and to serve us well. What we decide to do is not what everybody else does. Other companies sponsor women's events and put a woman's face in advertising. This is financial services wrapped in pink.

Lisa Caputo

My dream was to have my own advertising agency by the time I was 30, and that was before I got into movies.

John G. Avildsen

The Saudi government uses a lot of British equipment to suppress their own people. But we're happy for our politicians to go on advertising trips to Saudi, selling our weapons at the trade conventions.

Paul Conroy

I was taken in by what might be called the Hard Times version of the Communists' advertising or recruiting technique.

Elia Kazan

I was an accountant in Chicago, and a friend of mine, Ed Gallagher, was in advertising. At 4:30 every day I'd be bored, and I would call him. He'd interview me.

Bob Newhart

Advertising is the art of the tiny. You have to tell a complete a story and deliver a complete message in a very encapsulated form. It disciplines you to cut away extraneous information.

Dick Wolf

Advertising must respect the intelligence of its audience and if it does not prompt them to think, it will be instantly dismissed.

Maurice Saatchi

In advertising, I was frustrated by having to deal with the client. It was the only time I really worked in a proper office, and I didn't like it-simple as that.

Terry Gilliam

I am so spoiled. I cannot watch a show where it gets interrupted for ads. I have to TiVo it and skip through the ads, because the culture of advertising is so false and phony that I just... ugh, you know?

Alan Ball

Hammer down product fundamentals first. Make sure you've got something that works before doubling down on promotion and marketing. Create a groundswell of organic support, and only then leverage PR and advertising to spread the word.

Ryan Holmes

We think we have to work because the advertising industry has elevated wants into needs. The newspapers and the television batter us incessantly with the latest 'must-haves', whether that's shoes, videogames or patio heaters. As a result, mums think they 'have' to work at Tesco in order to buy expensive trainers.

Tom Hodgkinson

I think video advertising is a hugely compelling medium.

Susan Wojcicki

I think that my peers deserve more than products to buy wrapped up in advertising. We need ideas to share and causes to believe in - opportunities to lead and teach.

Adora Svitak

The simplest definition of advertising, and one that will probably meet the test of critical examination, is that advertising is selling in print.

Daniel Starch

Advertising as the printed form of selling would seem... ultimately to be justified in so far as it serves as a means of increasing legitimate human wants, as an agency of fair and economic competition in the distribution of goods, and as a stimulant to social progress.

Daniel Starch

I had been keeping an off eye on the advertising field, thinking I might become an idea man and a copywriter.

Carl Sandburg

I could live very quietly, do advertising to earn money.

Carine Roitfeld

I became an art major, took every art class my school had to offer. In college, I majored in Advertising Art and Design.

Len Wein

Editorial outfits are now advertising agencies.

Tina Brown

I come out of TV. I come out of live television, BBC drama: that's where I started first as a designer, then a director. Then I went independent TV, then television advertising.

Ridley Scott

News represents another form of advertising, not liberal propaganda.

Christopher Lasch

There's so much truly putrid advertising out there it's embarrassing. But not all advertising is bad. Some of it is really quite mediocre.

Jef I. Richards

Obviously the commercial news media tries to get you worked up and terrified so you'll buy products that they're advertising.

Matt Taibbi

When you break it down, Yahoo! is a Very Large Display Advertising business, with a hefty side of search and a bit of this and that on top.

John Battelle

Everyone dies, and before that, most people eventually lose some of their faculties. So some people worry that as marketers get better at targeting the elderly, the line between advertising and unscrupulous manipulation will be harder to discern.

Charles Duhigg

During the 1960s, the Shanghai of my childhood seemed a portent of the media cities of the future, dominated by advertising and mass circulation newspapers and swept by unpredictable violence.

J. G. Ballard

Advertising is the genie which is transforming America into a place of comfort, luxury and ease for millions.

William Allen White

Especially when you are advertising a product, I talk to the photographer and we create a character - it always gives you more freedom because it makes it less about yourself.

Penelope Cruz

Free is not going to go away. Either the advertising model will still work, or there will still be literally hundreds of millions of people who want to put their information on the Net and want people to have access to it.

Vint Cerf

I think of Google as a set of overlapping things. It's a consumer platform, consumer phenomenon of which search is its fundamental activity, but there are many other things you can do than search... I think of Google as an advertising company who services the broader advertising industry in the ways that you know.

Eric Schmidt

Yahoo! is the only company with both scale and leadership in branded and search advertising.

Terry Semel

I walked out with 14 advertising projects.

Peter Max

Increasingly, it's actresses doing the big fashion advertising campaigns, and now there's no distinction between actresses and models.

Romola Garai

Language thus becomes monumental because of the mutations of advertising.

Robert Smithson

Trends in circulation and advertising - the rise of the Internet, which has made the daily newspaper look slow and unresponsive; the advent of Craigslist, which is wiping out classified advertising-have created a palpable sense of doom.

Eric Alterman

Advertising in the past has been predicated on a mass market and a captive audience.

Howard Rheingold

One thing we didn't know in 1996 is that it's very, very difficult, if not impossible, to sustain a culture with online advertising.

Howard Rheingold

Boxes and rectangles on the side or top of a website simply do not deliver against brand advertising goals. Like it or not, boxes and rectangles have for the most part become the province of direct response advertising, or brand advertising that pays, on average, as if it's driven by direct response metrics.

John Battelle

I am responsible for creating and overseeing the future products that make up Google Advertising.

Susan Wojcicki

I mean, you can't have advertising be the only official business of the information economy if the information economy is going to take over.

Jaron Lanier

I think you will see a point where the traditional model of advertising on TV or advertising online will go, and advertisers will cover one programme, no matter what platform it's being broadcast on. You'll see the same ads whether you are watching it on your TV, your computer or your phone.

Chad Hurley

We were the first people to do advertising on the Web. I actually saw in 1993 that the ad could be the content, the destination.

Tim O'Reilly

On some planet, I probably could have been a lawyer. On some planet, I could have been somebody in advertising.

Stone Gossard

There is a huge difference between journalism and advertising. Journalism aspires to truth. Advertising is regulated for truth. I'll put the accuracy of the average ad in this country up against the average news story any time.

Jef I. Richards

I have turned down so many major advertising bids because I think either the time isn't right or I'm not.

Linda Evangelista

The Internet and Yahoo are firmly established as 'must buys' for brand advertising.

Terry Semel

I worked at Military Media, an advertising agency for military-base newspapers. Don't ask, I won't tell.

Judy Gold

The dark comedies tend to be in a non-releasable area. There can be romantic comedies. There can be dramas. But there's no 'dark comedy' inbox for the advertising.

Gus Van Sant

I'm an optimist. I hope if a movie's good that it will be a success, but as we know, that's not always true, just because of popular taste, advertising, distribution patterns - there's lots of reasons.

Willem Dafoe

First there's my role just as an executive being responsible for advertising, regardless of gender. I think that's a position that I take seriously. That's the first role. But I think for my role as a woman at Google, you try to set a good example and be a role model for the other women in the organization.

Susan Wojcicki

Google is a consumer brand and people need to be comfortable. If we were just an advertising brand we wouldn't have the same concerns. We've always tried to promote transparency and choice among our users.

Susan Wojcicki

Now with the Internet, a celebrity is fair game, and it's all designed to sell advertising space.

Randy Quaid

Newspapers are not free and they never have been. They can appear to be so, but someone, somewhere is covering the costs whether that is through advertising, a patron's largesse or a license fee. Advertising is no longer subsidising the industry and so the cost must fall somewhere - why not on the people who use it?

Heather Brooke

I have raced against the clock since I went into advertising at the age of eighteen.

Jan Karon

I wanted to be some kind of captain of industry. Then I wanted to be in advertising, and then I wanted to be a newspaper reporter.

Ken Follett

Marmite - like that other little black-jar job, Bovril - is so much a Mark 1 staple-of-Empire brand, so much part of the Edwardian world of enamel advertising signs, the history of grin-and-bear-it industrial food.

Peter York

I left advertising as fast as I could in 1961. And I haven't ever thought about going back.

Elmore Leonard

They say that Madison Avenue will only pay high dollars in advertising if they get the 18-35 age range.

Sharon Gless

We are pushing hard to find quality advertising clients.

Ben Nicholson

I never intended to become a commercial filmmaker in the first place. What I do requires time and experimentation. Commercial work is often not the best way to get the most innovative work, because it's about money and marketing. Although advertising is now embracing non-commercial people.

Marco Brambilla

I can't say the advertising model is obsolete yet but it doesn't make a lot of sense in the long range.

Jay Chiat

We should remember the campaign advertising will be only a smaller portion of the President's total exposure.

Robert Teeter

Most criticism of advertising is written in ignorance of what actually happens inside these agencies.

Michael Schudson

They're still advertising the added health-giving advantages of vitamins in your daily diet, although it has long since been shown that you'd be better off eating Smarties.

Terry Wogan

The business model for content is to be paid for it. You can be paid for it either though advertising or subscriptions or some new invention, but right now what we've got is advertising revenue and subscription revenue as the only way to be paid for content.

Barry Diller

The susceptibility of the average modern to pictorial suggestion enables advertising to exploit his lessened power of judgment.

Johan Huizinga

Google's thing is not advertising because it's not a romanticizing operation. It doesn't involve expression. It's a link. What they're doing is selling access.

Jaron Lanier

Nobody's profitable at this moment, because recession is on; advertising dollars are down, and expenses are way up. So that kind of belies the situation that you would expect, because the ratings are way up everywhere.

Brit Hume

Radio continues to be the very best advertising music performers have. No one who ever grabbed a Grammy got there without radio.

Gordon Smith

My background is advertising: I moved to New York from London in 1998 to start up the U.S. office of ad agency Bartle Bogle Hegarty.

Cindy Gallop

The only thing that really annoys me is when all of a sudden you hear yourself on the radio advertising Smith's tyre shop or Blenkinsop's jam. They simply can't do that. And in Australia, occasionally I have to take action.

Richie Benaud

In other words, if you - the cost of promoting movies, the advertising and promotion of a movie, the budget is almost as large as the cost of the movie.

Richard Attenborough

I think we have to recognize as an industry that users have a lot more choices and can click away to a lot more media. As a result, the advertising we create really needs to be something users want to see.

Susan Wojcicki

People used to say that advertising wasn't in Google's DNA, and that's obviously not true anymore. They used to say that display advertising isn't in Google's DNA, and that's not true any more.

Susan Wojcicki

Studies indicate that these children are more susceptible to advertising and even less likely to understand the purpose of this advertising.

Bob Filner

But in terms of the code by which we go to market - it's not telling kids to supersize, we're not selling them, generally, products, in the advertising we do to them.

Jim Cantalupo

I learned not to be so bitterly defeated when my fiction took a beating from editors. I learned in advertising to color in the lines and have my work done on time and to make it the very best it could be.

Jan Karon

My mother worked in advertising and my father was a journalist. But they split up when I was three and I grew up in a single-parent family. My mum brought my brother and I up.

Felicity Jones

I've never worked in advertising - my experience was as an editorial designer for magazines - but you could say, in the bigger picture, that magazines are vehicles for colour advertising.

Barbara Kruger

I feel the film companies should pay for proper advertising to
see that the movie will sell, instead of putting it on our backs.

Billy Crudup

I got my start in the 'New York Times' because I used to read
Stuart Elliot, the advertising columns. I still do. And I read him
so religiously, I wanted to work for him before I died.

Andrew Ross Sorkin

It is very likely that many firms spend more on advertising
than, for their own best interests, they should.

Michael Schudson

The trouble with us in America isn't that the poetry of life has
turned to prose, but that it has turned to advertising copy.

Louis Kronenberger

I get invited to premieres, and I've been to a few fashion shows
and stuff, but I always get really bored. I feel quite awkward.
You have to wear something by them, and it all feels like,
'Why am I doing free advertising for you?'

Bat for Lashes

We are not advertising ourselves as a secure platform. It's a communication platform. It's not our job to police the world or Snapchat of jerks.

Evan Spiegel

When executing advertising, it's best to think of yourself as an uninvited guest in the living room of a prospect who has the magical power to make you disappear instantly.

John O'Toole

I've devoted a lot of my time and effort during the past few years to developing my advertising copywriting business to the point of where I can support my family and don't have to depend on writing fiction for my income.

George Stephen

That's great advertising when you can turn Chicago into a city you'd want to spend more than three hours in.

Jerry Della Femina

When you invest in high-quality brands, it pays off with high-quality audiences and, ultimately, high-quality advertising rates.

Jim Bankoff

If advertising had a little more respect for the public, the public would have a lot more respect for advertising.

James Randolph Adams

Millions of dollars' worth of advertising shows such little respect for the reader's intelligence that it amounts almost to outright insult.

James Randolph Adams

The record labels used to spend money on advertising, and social media has replaced that entirely - it's putting magazines out of business. It's put big companies into completely reinventing their strategies.

Steve Aoki

A lot of the ways of advertising a book - the cover, whether somebody sees it on a subway or sees it in a bookstore - those things are going to rapidly diminish as we move to an electronic model.

Gary Shteyngart

These films however, have ambiguity built into them, because it's too easy in film to make a strident work of propaganda or advertising, which are really the same thing anyway, meaning the message is unmistakable.

Godfrey Reggio

Traditional media brand advertising is 65% to 70% spend; online, it's like 28%. You've got a huge margin.

Ross Levinsohn

Video will drive the share-shift in advertising.

Ross Levinsohn

Most people don't have the money to spend on advertising to create awareness among readers, nor do they have the contacts at newspapers or magazines to get their books reviewed.

Sara Paretsky

American advertisers rely on 'essentially illogical' approaches to determine their advertising budgets.

Michael Schudson

I'm always prepared for the worst. I was prepared to have the book come out, sell seven copies, and have to keep working in advertising, so it was just great that it was received so well and by such a huge audience.

Augusten Burroughs

I don't think there is enough educational programming, but unfortunately, television is built around advertising and those shows don't get the big ratings.

Will McDonough

I used to run record companies, and I went to the advertising business at 29 years old.

Steve Stoute

There's much more money being brought into the advertising and communications business than in the music industry.

Steve Stoute

Think of it: television producers joining with newspapers to tell stories. It's journalism of the future. Advertising will follow the crowd - the 'crowd' being viewers and readers, of course, which could bring revenue back into journalism.

Bill Kurtis

It's very possible that advertising business models will simply never do as well on mobile devices as those oriented around transactions.

Patrick Collison

If you look at the history of advertising, most of them were Jews, so it was only a matter of time before 'Mad Men' explored that area of advertising.

Ben Feldman

When comics came along in the 1930s there was a talent pool waiting. And one reason is so many areas were closed to Jews. Colleges, advertising agencies, many of the corporations - the doors that were closed led to the one that was open.

Jerry Robinson

Advertising seemed almost natural to me because it was a business where you had to inform, persuade and educate. And so from being a junior copywriter to being the creative director of one of the largest advertising agencies in the country took me 4.5 years, which is, well, a fairly spectacular rise.

Bryce Courtenay

Advertising was only meant to be a very small part of my life. I had intended that I would work extensively in journalism for about five or six years and then I'd become a writer.

Bryce Courtenay

'Brand-Dropping' is the term that the Kluger Agency coined to describe discreetly advertising by product mentioning in song, and we feel we can make this the way of the future without jeopardizing any artist's creative outlet or typical style.

Adam Kluger

I initially wanted to work in the music industry more on the A&R side. While I was in school, I began working in the New Business department of an advertising firm, and very quickly I was responsible for roughly 70% of their business, so you could say I had a natural knack for the advertising world.

Adam Kluger

If you want quality service, you have to pay for it. You don't buy into waste. I have great misgivings about the amount of advertising that we see in the health care field, some by hospitals, a lot by drug companies.

Dave Obey

I've set aside a nice chunk of my advertising revenue each month for giveaways, like a KitchenAid mixer. I like buying them for the audience, because without the audience I wouldn't have the blog or the revenue in the first place.

Ree Drummond

Personally, I'd love to see more social media firms develop business models that aren't reliant on advertising. If you're a social media firm selling ads, your goal is to get people to interrupt what they're doing all day long so they come and stare at your service as much as possible.

Clive Thompson

There is a pool of references in New York and Los Angeles that are almost exclusively drawn from the media, from the world of television and advertising.

Marshall Brickman

My concern is the really great concepts that are features, not companies. There isn't enough advertising to support all those features, and in compression times, advertisers tend to flock to safe names and sites that have real traction.

Ross Levinsohn

I was not going to use writing for advertising or journalism. I would tend bar, load trucks, chauffeur - do whatever it took. But from the moment I took my first writing workshop, I was a writer.

Dennis Lehane

Yes, I sell people things they don't need. I can't, however, sell them something they don't want. Even with advertising. Even if I were of a mind to.

John O'Toole

Is advertising moral? It is part and parcel of the American free enterprise system... I challenge anybody to show any economic system that has done as much for so many in so short a time.

Morris Hite

If advertising is not an official or state art, it is nonetheless clearly art.

Michael Schudson

In college, I majored - I can't believe there is such a thing - in advertising. And I worked in advertising and PR for a while, and I liked it.

Traylor Howard

I grew up in a country where advertising doesn't exist.

Jan Koum

There's no one I trust in show business more than Sabrina Wind. She's my eyes and ears when I can't be there. She weighs in on everything, from scripts to sets to advertising.

Marc Cherry

I'm really a strong advocate of ageing because the messages that the media and advertising give to women infuriate me: ie that it's a bad thing to get old.

Sophia Myles

If you had the opportunity and some talent, there was no way you couldn't progress, because it was an open market. There was the advertising world, and there was the documentary world.

Richard Donner

Taxpayers will not stand for - nor should they - the funding of poster sites, leaflets or advertising. What people will support is funding for political education, for training, for party organization.

Peter Hain

I decided to do advertising, as ad films were made in only 10 days, and started assisting Sanjeev Sharma and Mansoor Khan. Surprisingly, I was a whiz kid and soon learnt to edit films and became an expert at it.

Ronit Roy

I've spent some time working with a non-Italian designer; I've been helping him organize fashion shows, the advertising, also helping with the creative part. But the great part about this work is that I am no one!

Allegra Versace

Money is tighter now, with the advertising dollar spread a lot more thinly across a whole range of media because of the Internet. It means the television networks have less power to produce shows, and TV is where most Australian actors make their money.

Grant Bowler

The network and local TV angle of broadcast television has received a black eye for not properly debating within the news issues that should be debated, instead of shuffling them of to television advertising.

Mark E. Hyman

We make programming decisions on a day-to-day basis. We sell advertising on a day-to-day basis. This is the way networks operate. This is the way all television stations operate. This is the way most businesses operate when you have a number of affiliates or a number of franchises. It's the way the business operates.

Mark E. Hyman

There is no way for the American economic system to function without advertising. There is no other way to communicate enough information about enough products to enough people with enough speed.

John O'Toole

I don't want to kill ads. I think advertising is great, and I'm very aware that there's multiple revenue streams in television, subscription and advertising. But I also don't want to put my head in the sand, and I think the world is changing.

Charlie Ergen

'Be comfortable with who you are', reads the headline on the Hush Puppies poster. Are they mad? If people were comfortable with who they were, they'd never buy any products except the ones they needed, and then where would the advertising industry be?

Charles Edwards

Two common conceptions with regard to advertising which are held by a considerable number of people are that enormously large sums of money are expended for it, and that much of this expenditure is an economic waste.

Daniel Starch

Advertising gets such a bashing from the world. At parties you are always asked, 'Aren't you just selling people things they don't want?'

Paul Arden

Our phones are so intimately connected to us, to our lives. Putting advertising on a device like that is a bad idea. You don't want to be interrupted by ads when you're chatting with your loved ones.

Jan Koum

I began illustrating children's books because of a growing disillusionment with the sort of work I was doing in the advertising industry. Book publishing offered me the chance to be far more creative.

Graeme Base

I was always interested in art at school, and after year twelve, senior year, I spent three years studying graphic design at college. I worked in advertising for two years but didn't like it much, then began doing a bit of illustration work for various publishers.

Graeme Base

Online advertising is display plus search.

David Filo

I've been doing documentaries for about 25 years and want to continue to do that, but I love the idea of working in a different medium. Advertising pushes the envelope creatively, and there is some really great work being done right now, so I'm excited to jump into it.

Rory Kennedy

I have an architecture degree; that's what my college degree is in. And that sucked. I started doing Web and CD-ROM development really early on, and then that grew into being an art director and doing advertising work.

Jonathan Hickman

As a child, I wanted to go into advertising. I had a love affair with the advertising industry.

Nadezhda Tolokonnikova

'Flappy Bird' was one of those phenomena. If we could all build one now, we would. Probably a bunch of us are trying.

Those kinds of games are interesting. Rumor has it he was making $50,000 a day just from advertising, which is great, especially given the cost of living in Vietnam.

Chris DeWolfe

The strategy is obviously a business decision to have limited advertising on the WWE Network. We want subscribers to know that there won't be commercial breaks during scheduled programming, so your shows won't be interrupted.

Stephanie McMahon

What we'd like to think of YouTube as is a part of Google with very overlapping goals and values. We're a fundamental part of the advertising business for Google.

Salar Kamangar

When two kids came along, I couldn't see how I could support them. The way it played out, I was away from the theatre for five years. I was a postie for the first part and then worked as an advertising copywriter, but I somehow found my way back.

Peter Hambleton

Advertising is legalized lying.

H. G. Wells

Advertising people who ignore research are as dangerous as generals who ignore decodes of enemy signals.

David Ogilvy

Nothing except the mint can make money without advertising.

Thomas Babington Macaulay

Advertising is the very essence of democracy.

Anton Chekhov

While it may be true that the best advertising is word-of-mouth, never lose sight of the fact it also can be the worst advertising.

Jef I. Richards

The secret of all effective advertising is not the creation of new and tricky words and pictures, but one of putting familiar words and pictures into new relationships.

Leo Burnett

I'm going to do all my movies here in Chicago. The 'Tribune' referred to me as a 'former Chicagoan.' As if, to do anything, I had to leave Chicago. I never left. I worked until I was 29 at the Leo Burnett advertising agency, and then I quit to do this. This is a working city, where people go to their jobs and raise their kids and live their lives.

John Hughes

American culture is probably the least Christian culture that we've ever had because it is so materialistic and it's so full of lies. The whole advertising world is just, it's just intertwined with lies, appealing to the worst of the instincts we have.

Eugene H. Peterson

Advertising is a business of words, but advertising agencies are infested with men and women who cannot write. They cannot write advertisements, and they cannot write plans. They are helpless as deaf mutes on the stage of the Metropolitan Opera.

David Ogilvy

You can tell the ideals of a nation by its advertising.

Norman Douglas

Chess is as elaborate a waste of human intelligence as you can find outside an advertising agency.

Raymond Chandler

In the arts, the critic is the only independent source of information. The rest is advertising.

Pauline Kael

It is not unprofessional to give free legal advice, but advertising that the first visit will be free is a bit like a fox telling chickens he will not bite them until they cross the threshold of the hen house.

Warren E. Burger

News is what somebody somewhere wants to suppress; all the rest is advertising.

Lord Northcliffe

Ensure your employees understand what your brand stands for so they can be your first line of word-of-mouth advertising.

Simon Mainwaring

Advertising moves people toward goods; merchandising moves goods toward people.

Morris Hite

Ideally, advertising aims at the goal of a programmed harmony among all human impulses and aspirations and endeavors. Using handicraft methods, it stretches out toward the ultimate electronic goal of a collective consciousness.

Marshall McLuhan

The sole purpose of business is service. The sole purpose of advertising is explaining the service which business renders.

Leo Burnett

The advent of Google+ and the emergence of the personalized web means this is more true than ever. Brands, and their advertising partners, must wake up to this challenge and define themselves with clarity, consistency and authenticity. Otherwise they just might find themselves shouting in a ghost town.

Simon Mainwaring

I'm Phil Knight, and I don't believe in advertising.

Phil Knight

Let advertisers spend the same amount of money improving their product that they do on advertising and they wouldn't have to advertise it.

Will Rogers

It is the advertiser who provides the paper for the subscriber. It is not to be disputed, that the publisher of a newspaper in this country, without a very exhaustive advertising support, would receive less reward for his labor than the humblest mechanic.

Alexander Hamilton

Advertising says to people, 'Here's what we've got. Here's what it will do for you. Here's how to get it.'

Leo Burnett

You go on Facebook, you buy social advertising. And you can very cost-effectively target people who are in the market for your product from all over the world.

Marc Andreesen

Today's smartest advertising style is tomorrow's corn.

William Bernbach

Social enables word of mouth at an unprecedented scale. Its most powerful effect, through reviews and recommendations, is to put product quality and value for money as the key to success in commerce. Social brings a level of transparency that prevents marketers from advertising their way to success without underlying product quality.

Roelof Botha

Advertising, music, atmospheres, subliminal messages and films can have an impact on our emotional life, and we cannot control it because we are not even conscious of it.

Tariq Ramadan

It is advertising and the logic of consumerism that governs the depiction of reality in the mass media.

Christopher Lasch

The work of an advertising agency is warmly and immediately human. It deals with human needs, wants, dreams and hopes. Its 'product' cannot be turned out on an assembly line.

Leo Burnett

Anyone who thinks that people can be fooled or pushed around has an inaccurate and pretty low estimate of people - and he won't do very well in advertising.

Leo Burnett

Driving up the value of the advertising is a big commitment for Microsoft.

Bill Gates

Advertising is the rattling of a stick inside a swill bucket.

George Orwell

I saw a subliminal advertising executive, but only for a second.

Steven Wright

Advertising: the science of arresting the human intelligence long enough to get money from it.

Stephen Leacock

I've done a number of Super Bowl ads. And that is the best advertising of the year. That is when people realize they're going to be compared directly against other ads.

Jerry Seinfeld

In advertising, not to be different is virtual suicide.

Thornton Wilder

Advertising is a valuable economic factor because it is the cheapest way of selling goods, particularly if the goods are worthless.

Sinclair Lewis

It is pretty obvious that the debasement of the human mind caused by a constant flow of fraudulent advertising is no trivial thing. There is more than one way to conquer a country.

Raymond Chandler

Advertising is the ability to sense, interpret... to put the very heart throbs of a business into type, paper and ink.

Leo Burnett

When air conditioning, escalators, and advertising appeared, shopping expanded its scale, but also limited its spontaneity. And it became much more predictable, almost scientific. What had once been the most surprising became the most manipulated.

Rem Koolhaas

Advertising generally works to reinforce consumer trends rather than to initiate them.

Michael Schudson

We are a consumer company and our success is directly linked to our users trusting us. Therefore we have the same incentive as the user: they want to see relevant advertising so their experience of Google is positive and we want to deliver it.

Susan Wojcicki

What is the difference between unethical and ethical advertising? Unethical advertising uses falsehoods to deceive the public; ethical advertising uses truth to deceive the public.

Vilhjalmur Stefansson

Advertising is the life of trade.

Calvin Coolidge

Any time an investment company has to spend heavily on advertising, it's probably a bad business in which to invest.

Robert Kiyosaki

The philosophy behind much advertising is based on the old observation that every man is really two men - the man he is and the man he wants to be.

William Feather

History will see advertising as one of the real evil things of our time. It is stimulating people constantly to want things, want this, want that.

Malcolm Muggeridge

Appropriation is the idea that ate the art world. Go to any Chelsea gallery or international biennial and you'll find it. It's there in paintings of photographs, photographs of advertising, sculpture with ready-made objects, videos using already-existing film.

Jerry Saltz

Month after month, Wizard Academy equips people who want to make a difference. This is why journalists and scientists and artists and educators and business owners and advertising professionals and ministers are attracted to our little school.

Roy H. Williams

Censorship is advertising paid by the government.

Federico Fellini

The truth is that our way of celebrating the Christmas season does spring from myriad cultures and sources, from St. Nicholas to Coca-Cola advertising campaigns.

Richard Roeper

Forget words like 'hard sell' and 'soft sell.' That will only confuse you. Just be sure your advertising is saying something with substance, something that will inform and serve the consumer, and be sure you're saying it like it's never been said before.

William Bernbach

I wish all consumers were as gullible as advertising's biggest critics. Anyone who believes advertising is that powerful will believe almost anything.

Jef I. Richards

Advertising is totally unnecessary. Unless you hope to make money.

Jef I. Richards

In my first start-up, I had an initial advertising budget of $5 per day total. That would buy us 100 clicks per day. At $5 per day, marketing people scoffed and said that is too small to matter. But if you think about it, to an engineer, 100 real humans everyday giving your product a try means you can really start improving.

Eric Ries

There was a period of time in America where the advertising world actually went to the housewives of America and had them write jingles that would appeal to them. It was actually brilliant marketing.

Julianne Moore

The only prejudice I've found anywhere in TV is in some advertising agencies, and there isn't so much prejudice as just fear.

Nat King Cole

If advertisers spent the same amount of money on improving their products as they do on advertising then they wouldn't have to advertise them.

Will Rogers

Advertising treats all products with the reverence and the seriousness due to sacraments.

Thomas Merton

My mom was a single mother, raising my sister and me. My mom has an incredible talent for living in the world without traditional structure, and her friend, who was in advertising, put me in a commercial when I was five. It was just to make money.

Gaby Hoffmann

I started selling out comedy clubs before I got to town with no advertising. I was selling out theaters just on the rumor that I was going to be there.

Ron White

Mass demand has been created almost entirely through the development of advertising.

Calvin Coolidge

Kindle Singles is publishing on skates. It prints like lightning; our book meets readers in hours. I've spent so many years waiting for publishers to consider whether they wanted to print a book of mine, making contracts, taking months to fit it into the Fall list or the Spring list, fitting it into an advertising plan.

Richard Bach

Advertising ministers to the spiritual side of trade. It is great power that has been entrusted to your keeping which charges you with the high responsibility of inspiring and ennobling the commercial world. It is all part of the greater work of the regeneration and redemption of mankind.

Calvin Coolidge

Advertising is a racket, like the movies and the brokerage business. You cannot be honest without admitting that its constructive contribution to humanity is exactly minus zero.

F. Scott Fitzgerald

A tremendous amount of the entrepreneurial initiative, if you want to call it that, comes from the dynamic state sector on which most of the economy relies to socialize costs and risks and privatize eventual profit. And that's achieved by, if you like, advertising.

Noam Chomsky

An advertising agency is 85 percent confusion and 15 percent commission.

Fred Allen

Advertising is the modern substitute for argument; its function is to make the worse appear the better.

George Santayana

Until the rise of American advertising, it never occurred to anyone anywhere in the world that the teenager was a captive in a hostile world of adults.

Gore Vidal

Political advertising ought to be stopped. It's the only really dishonest kind of advertising that's left. It's totally dishonest.

David Ogilvy

A lot of advertising has gotten worse. I think it's kind of lost its nerve, to be honest with you. I feel like the advertising of the '60s, they were nervier. You know why? Because there was less at stake.

Jerry Seinfeld

It used to be that a fellow went on the police force when everything else failed, but today he goes in the advertising game.

Kin Hubbard

The vice-president of an advertising agency is a bit of executive fungus that forms on a desk that has been exposed to conference.

Fred Allen

Advertising is an environmental striptease for a world of abundance.

Marshall McLuhan

Advertising is salesmanship mass produced. No one would bother to use advertising if he could talk to all his prospects face-to-face. But he can't.

Morris Hite

Can advertising foist an inferior product on the consumer? Bitter experience has taught me that it cannot. On those rare occasions when I have advertised products which consumer tests have found inferior to other products in the same field, the results have been disastrous.

David Ogilvy

Every night I watch the nightly news. It's funded by the pharmaceutical companies. Virtually every ad is a drug ad. They get their say every night on the nightly news through advertising.

Michael Moore

Marriage is a good deal like a circus: there is not as much in it as is represented in the advertising.

E. W. Howe

I can not think of any circumstances in which advertising would not be an evil.

Arnold J. Toynbee

The relationship between a manufacturer and his advertising agency is almost as intimate as the relationship between a patient and his doctor. Make sure that you can life happily with your prospective client before you accept his account.

David Ogilvy

Governing today means giving acceptable signs of credibility. It is like advertising and it is the same effect that is achieved - commitment to a scenario.

Jean Baudrillard

Much of the messy advertising you see on television today is the product of committees. Committees can criticize advertisements, but they should never be allowed to create them.

David Ogilvy

Leave America and you'll find that the consumers in many other countries enjoy watching advertising. Not because the products are better, but because the ads are produced to be entertaining. Sometimes they are funny. Sometimes they are dramatic. Sometimes they are just beautiful.

Simon Sinek

I have been asked what would I ban immediately if I could. Advertising.

Vivienne Westwood

Many manufacturers secretly question whether advertising really sells their product, but are vaguely afraid that their competitors might steal a march on them if they stopped.

David Ogilvy

There are very few men of genius in advertising agencies. But we need all we can find. Almost without exception they are disagreeable. Don't destroy them. They lay golden eggs.

David Ogilvy

Google did a great job hacking the Web to create search - and then monetizing search with advertising. And Apple did a great job humanizing hardware and software so that formerly daunting computers and applications could become consumer-friendly devices - even a lifestyle brand.

Douglas Rushkoff

The very first law in advertising is to avoid the concrete promise and cultivate the delightfully vague.

Stuart Chase

While Google no longer has a search engine operation inside China, it has maintained a large presence in Beijing and Shanghai focused on research and development, advertising sales, and mobile platform development.

Rebecca MacKinnon

Society drives people crazy with lust and calls it advertising.

John Lahr

Advertising is, of course, important because advertise is the final design. It's the last layer that speaks to the customer, that tells them what you have.

Tom Ford

Have you heard of this new thing called the internet? It's giving people new expectations. It's allowing them to become their own expert. Knowledge lies anxious at their fingertips. Gloss over the truth in your advertising and you'll quickly be dismissed as a poser.

Roy H. Williams

The secret of all effective originality in advertising is not the creation of new and tricky words and pictures, but one of putting familiar words and pictures into new relationships.

Leo Burnett

Neoclassical economics insists that advertising cannot force consumers to buy anything they don't already want to buy.

Christopher Lasch

Here is what the practical impact of Citizens United means. What Citizens United means is that corporations call hundreds of millions of dollars into television ads, radio ads, and other forms of advertising to defeat those candidates who stand up and take them on.

Bernie Sanders

While Google has given away pretty much everything it has to offer - from search and maps to email and apps - this has always been part of its greater revenue model: the pennies per placement it gets for seeding the entire Google universe of search and services with ever more targeted advertising.

Douglas Rushkoff

My mother is a special education teacher but also an artist, and my father an advertising executive. They are about as wacky as you can get without being alcoholics.

Sloane Crosley

Somebody says, 'Do a Tom Bodett, a folksy kind of thing,' and it sounds like something out of 'Hee Haw,' very insulting. They turn wry humor into disparaging sarcasm, and you get what amounts to insulting advertising.

Tom Bodett

In the world of commercial speech, tobacco advertising bears the earmarks of an endangered species.

Jef I. Richards

Any seeming deception in a statement is costly, not only in the expense of the advertising but in the detrimental effect produced upon the customer, who believes she has been misled.

John Wanamaker

Advertising doesn't create a product advantage. It can only convey it.

William Bernbach

Regardless of the moral issue, dishonesty in advertising has proved very unprofitable.

Leo Burnett

Despite all the public hand-wringing about negative advertising, political veterans will tell you that it persists because, more often than not, it works. But tearing down the other guy has another attraction: It can be a substitute for building much of a case for what the mudslinger will do once in office.

Robert Dallek

Publishing is a very mysterious business. It is hard to predict what kind of sale or reception a book will have, and advertising seems to do very little good.

Thomas Wolfe

We grew up founding our dreams on the infinite promise of American advertising. I still believe that one can learn to play the piano by mail and that mud will give you a perfect complexion.

Zelda Fitzgerald

The funny thing about advertising is that it's not a zero-sum game... Historically, in the digital ad world, pie has gotten larger and it's possible for everyone to win, and it's perfectly possible that will continue to be true for quite some time.

Eric Schmidt

We have always said that advertising is just the icing on the cake. It is not the cake.

Meg Whitman

One of the big no-nos in cyberspace is that you do not go into a social activity, a chat group or something like that, and start advertising or selling things. This etiquette rule is an attempt to separate one's social life, which should be pure enjoyment and relaxation, from the pressures of work.

Judith Martin

If your advertising goes unnoticed, everything else is academic.

William Bernbach

I understand that I have a certain look that can be used to my advantage. I know the power of that when I walk into a room and talk to people, and I can use it as an advertising tool. Now I am actually selling me, my face, my thoughts. So I am my guy.

Tom Ford

Just advertising departments with legs and high heels.

Richard Avedon

There are always protests, whether you do something good or bad. Even if you do something beneficial, people say you do it because it's advertising.

Giorgio Armani

Advertising is, actually, a simple phenomenon in terms of economics. It is merely a substitute for a personal sales force - an extension, if you will, of the merchant who cries aloud his wares.

Rosser Reeves

There is no such thing as a permanent advertising success.

Leo Burnett

You really want to get a headache? Try to understand Internet advertising.

Barry Diller

While working in advertising, I channelled my creative energy into elaborate escape fantasies: cake making, dog breeding, the Peace Corps.

Meg Rosoff

Advertising and content have always been bound together - in print, on television, and on the web. Sure, you can skip the ad - just flip the page, or press 'ffwd' on your DVR. But great advertising, as I've long argued, adds value to the content ecosystem, and has as much a right to be in the conversation as does the publisher and the consumer.

John Battelle

I wrote for magazines. I wrote adventure stuff, I wrote for the 'National Enquirer,' I wrote advertising copy for cemeteries.

Walter Dean Myers

If Chevy Chase had not been an actor, he might have been a very popular guy in advertising or whatever field he would have gone into, because of his charisma.

Harold Ramis

If you're running an engineering or finance company, all companies depend on ideas and ingenuity. I think the principles of creative leadership apply everywhere, whether it's an advertising company or whether you're running a hospital.

Ken Robinson

People don't understand the logistics of advertising. To have the ads purchased and run, you need to have a series of products that work together.

Susan Wojcicki

More traffic means more advertising dollars.

Jeff Zucker

Vertical search engines that match your business, service or products with a target market offer you a higher conversion rate than traditional search engines. Because they have already qualified their interest by coming to a search engine with a specific focus, searchers will be more receptive to targeted advertising.

Marc Ostrofsky

Poetry is a street fighter. It has sharp elbows. It can look after itself. Poetry can't be used for manipulation; it's why you never see good poetry in advertising.

David Whyte

I went to UCF in Florida in Orlando. I went for advertising and public relations. I moved out to California my senior year because I knew I wanted to be an actor, but I also wanted to finish school and get my degree. I took mainly a bunch of criminal justice courses online for the last year because that's all that they offered.

Drew Seeley

I honestly believe that advertising is the most fun you can have with your clothes on.

Jerry Della Femina

I didn't think that a career in theater was very realistic so I thought the only thing I could make money doing and still be somewhat artistic was, god help me, advertising.

Liev Schreiber

We do not invest in advertising... So racing is the best advertising for Ferrari.

Luca Cordero di Montezemolo

The Great Idea in advertising is far more than the sum of the recognition scores, the ratings and all the other superficial indicators of its success; it is in the realm of myth, to which measurements cannot apply.

Leo Bogart

NC-17 means that you get it in like 3 theaters. They won't run the spots on MTV, won't run the advertising. It's the kiss of death so there was really no other choice.

Rob Zombie

I think the adoption rate with respect to social media and how companies leverage that varies by the company. Cisco is probably a leader in the space. A lot of times, we actually use virtual ways to communicate our brand and do some of our advertising, first on the social space, then we do on physical advertising.

Padmasree Warrior

I view advertising as being this romanticizing element that helps us appreciate, understand and enjoy how remarkable it is that we've been able to do so much, and learn so much. I view it as really vital, even though sometimes it can be really annoying.

Jaron Lanier

There is a great deal of advertising that is much better than the product. When that happens, all that the good advertising will do is put you out of business faster.

Jerry Della Femina

Although it may seem callous to say so, millions of Americans are lucky that Magic Johnson was infected with H.I.V. There is no way of calculating how many lives he has saved. No advertising agency could have invented a better, or more effective, role model.

Michael Specter

It takes good clients to make a good advertising agency. Regardless of how much talent an ad agency may have, it is ineffective without good products and services to advertise.

Morris Hite

I have to admit I've always had quite a complex relationship with modeling and with the idea of advertising: not always knowing what I'm advertising and selling.

Lily Cole

My wife, Jill, and I have an incredibly close working relationship, and an incredibly happy married one. We met through work. I was the world's worst advertising copywriter. She had the misfortune to be my account director, so from the very start she was my boss, and she still is.

Anthony Horowitz

In fact, I argue that the future of advertising, whatever the technology, will be to associate each brand with one word. This is one word equity. It's the modern equivalent of having the best site on the high street, except the location is in the mind.

Maurice Saatchi

This hype word bothers me though It always sounds like an accusation, what does it mean, advertising, column inches in the press? Bands themselves are never really responsible for all of that. That is something that happens to you when you sell millions of records.

Holly Johnson

I was 15 when I got my first job as a proofreader for an advertising agency in the City, earning £12 a week. But by then, I was already playing darts tournaments every weekend, regularly winning the £50 first prize. By the time I was 16 and winning two or three contests a weekend, I ditched the agency job and concentrated on darts.

Eric Bristow

Advertising isn't just the disruption of aesthetics, the insults to your intelligence and the interruption of your train of thought. At every company that sells ads, a significant portion of their engineering team spends their day tuning data mining, writing better code to collect all your personal data.

Jan Koum

There are rules in advertising, and those rules are self-imposed by the client companies because they don't want their products to be seen as dishonest.

Paul Arden

When I first started writing, I was in advertising at the time, I was doing most of my writing on weekends. I had studied most of the other series heroes and I figured it would be fun for mine to be different and put him in and around water. So I dreamed up Dirk Pitt.

Clive Cussler

Like a midwife, I make my living bringing new babies into the world, except that mine are new advertising campaigns.

David Ogilvy

I know half the money I spend on advertising is wasted, but I can never find out which half.

John Wanamaker

What is your Unique Selling Proposition? What makes you different than your competitors? Wrap your advertising message around that USP and communicate it in a clear and concise manner.

Lynda Resnick

Certainly, it seems true enough that there's a good deal of irony in the world... I mean, if you live in a world full of politicians and advertising, there's obviously a lot of deception.

Kenneth Koch

You know why Madison Avenue advertising has never done well in Harlem? We're the only ones who know what it means to be Brand X.

Dick Gregory

As I see it, fast food outfits have targeted small children with their advertising in a very effective way. You know, it's clowns and kid's toys and bright colors and things like that.

Anthony Bourdain

They wouldn't play my records on American radio because I had spiky hair. They said, 'Punk rock doesn't sell advertising, it won't make any money.'

Billy Idol

Outside of advertising, the person who's influenced me most is quite possibly Frank Gehry.

Jay Chiat

The forced influence of advertising has given us completely useless TV. You don't want that on the Net. But most on-line information providers need to attract advertising - which slows download times and clutters the screen with windows.

Robert Cailliau

The future of advertising is the Internet.

Bill Gates

I'd like my grandkids to be able to watch PBS. But I'm not willing to borrow money from China, and make my kids have to pay the interest on that, and my grandkids, over generations, as opposed to saying to PBS, 'Look, you're going to have to raise more money from charitable contributions or from advertising.'

Mitt Romney

Advertising is only evil when it advertises evil things.

David Ogilvy

Expensive advertising courts us with hints and images. The ordinary kind merely says, Buy.

Mason Cooley

The force of the advertising word and image dwarfs the power of other literature in the 20th century.

Daniel J. Boorstin

The advertising world had space men in it before spacemen existed.

Fred Allen

I do not regard advertising as entertainment or an art form, but as a medium of information.

David Ogilvy

Advertising reflects the mores of society, but it does not influence them.

David Ogilvy

I don't read my books, I write them. Once I've finished the many years it usually takes me to write them, I can't bear to read them, because I've spent too long with them already. I'm not advertising them very well, am I?

Salman Rushdie

I avoid clients for whom advertising is only a marginal factor in their marketing mix. They have an awkward tendency to raid their advertising appropriations whenever they need cash for other purposes.

David Ogilvy

I always loved advertising. If I hadn't been in fashion, I'd have been in advertising.

Karl Lagerfeld

What you say in advertising is more important than how you say it.

David Ogilvy

A good basic selling idea, involvement and relevancy, of course, are as important as ever, but in the advertising din of today, unless you make yourself noticed and believed, you ain't got nothin'.

Leo Burnett

Does advertising corrupt editors? Yes it does, but fewer editors than you may suppose... the vast majority of editors are incorruptible.

David Ogilvy

Advertising has done more to cause the social unrest of the 20th century than any other single factor.

Clare Boothe Luce

Ninety-nine percent of advertising doesn't sell much of anything.

David Ogilvy

The headline is the 'ticket on the meat.' Use it to flag down readers who are prospects for the kind of product you are advertising.

David Ogilvy

It is flagrantly dishonest for an advertising agent to urge consumers to buy a product which he would not allow his own wife to buy.

David Ogilvy

The irony is, the advertising industry knows everyone hates what they produce. This is why they keep looking for new ways to force people to stay tuned.

Simon Sinek

Contrary to popular belief, Americans don't hate advertising.

Roy H. Williams

I warn you against believing that advertising is a science.

William Bernbach

The most important word in the vocabulary of advertising is TEST. If you pretest your product with consumers, and pretest your advertising, you will do well in the marketplace.

David Ogilvy

Remove advertising, disable a person or firm from proclaiming its wares and their merits, and the whole of society and of the economy is transformed. The enemies of advertising are the enemies of freedom.

David Ogilvy

Some manufacturers illustrate their advertisements with abstract paintings. I would only do this if I wished to conceal from the reader what I was advertising.

David Ogilvy

As advertising blather becomes the nation's normal idiom, language becomes printed noise.

George Will

I have learned that it is far easier to write a speech about good advertising than it is to write a good ad.

Leo Burnett

I am one who believes that one of the greatest dangers of advertising is not that of misleading people, but that of boring them to death.

Leo Burnett

The greatest thing to be achieved in advertising, in my opinion, is believability, and nothing is more believable than the product itself.

Leo Burnett

Advertising is the edge of what people know how to do and of human experience and it explains the latest ways progress has changed us to ourselves.

Jaron Lanier

One of the unintended negative consequences of online advertising has been the loss of value in traditional classifieds. It's simply quicker, simply easier for an end user who's online, on a broadband connection, to look things up and to figure out what they want to buy.

Eric Schmidt

I won't do advertising if they bring a layout and say, 'This is what we want to do,' because anybody can do that; it's not interesting. They've got digital and the computer; it's not taking pictures, it's not magic - it's a picture done by committee.

David Bailey

Some people have a taboo about doing advertising in the States. You know, where they kind of make their bread and butter. But to me, that's crazy.

Ice Cube

The reason advertising is governed by fear, after all, is that most agencies rely on just a few clients to bring in the lion's share of their revenues.

James Surowiecki

America is one of few advanced nations that allow direct advertising of prescription drugs.

Robert Reich

Online advertising may not be much more successful than an old double-barrel, but - like a good spray of buckshot - it makes up for its lack of accuracy with sheer volume. There are 10 unique ads listed with every Gmail message in your queue, each tied to the message content. And a paying sponsor.

Douglas Rushkoff

Back in the day I was doing runway, editorial, advertising, spokesmodeling, and public appearances. Those are five different categories.

Janice Dickinson

When the vast baby-boom generation exploded into adolescence in the 1960s, marketers exulted. Advertising consultants, always eager to coin a phrase, began happily explaining to corporations the difference between 'teenyboppers' and 'counterculture consumers.'

Charles Duhigg

I have learned that trying to guess what the boss or the client wants is the most debilitating of all influences in the creation of good advertising.

Leo Burnett

In our factory, we make lipstick. In our advertising, we sell hope.

Peter Nivio Zarlenga

Display advertising and the movies, though they may dull the wits, certainly stimulate the eyes.

John Dos Passos

A lot of consumers actively enjoy advertising, especially fashion print ads and clever TV commercials. The nostalgic cable channel TVLand features not only vintage shows but also vintage commercials.

Virginia Postrel

Sanely applied advertising could remake the world.

Stuart Chase

Advertising has always been a huge unrecognised source of outdoor relief for the arts.

Peter York

Great designers seldom make great advertising men, because they get overcome by the beauty of the picture - and forget that merchandise must be sold.

James Randolph Adams

Creativity is an advertising agency's most valuable asset, because it is the rarest.

Jef I. Richards

The Internet creates as well as destroys. Social networks, search advertising, and cloud computing are multibillion dollar industries that didn't exist 10 years ago. They are products of the same force that has rendered the Postal Service's core business obsolete.

John Sununu

Advertising men and politicians are dangerous if they are separated. Together they are diabolical.

Phillip Adams

Telling lies does not work in advertising.

Stanislaw Jerzy Lec